T0207723

YAH's Book of Psalms

For I shall proclaim the name of YAH,
Oh, tell the greatness of Our Creator! —
Deuteronomy 32:3 (New Jerusalem Bible)

Jabari Woods

WESTBOW
PRESS®
A DIVISION OF THOMAS NELSON
& ZONDERVAN

WestBow Press books may be ordered through booksellers or by contacting:

WestBow Press
A Division of Thomas Nelson & Zondervan
1663 Liberty Drive
Bloomington, IN 47403
www.westbowpress.com
1 (866) 928-1240

ISBN: 978-1-9736-7385-9 (sc)
ISBN: 978-1-9736-7387-3 (hc)
ISBN: 978-1-9736-7386-6 (e)

Library of Congress Control Number: 2019913352

Print information available on the last page.

WestBow Press rev. date: 12/30/2019

YAH Speaks Life ...

(Bonnie Woods and Jabari Woods,
Saturday, February 9, 2013)

Heart beating inside the cocoon of a woman's womb, time ticking in anticipation of the arrival of a special new soul. Oh come child of YAH into the universe YAH preordained for you from the foundation of the world....Oh come mother, daughter, sister, wife. Come to YAH's house of protection.

YAH is calling you to come. Come to YAH'S House of protection. Come to YAH'S house of love. Come to ABBA YAH'S House of Refuge. Come to YAH'S house and be safe.

Let the little children come to me, and do not hinder them, for the kingdom of heaven belongs to such as these. (Matthew 19:14 NIV)

Witness

(Written in YAHshua to YAH's glory
Tuesday, March 18, 2008, 1:47 p.m.)

Abba YAH, I share your name with others because I truly believe in you. I utter your words of life because I have found them to be so powerful, faithful, and true. I love your ways, Oh Ancient of Days. YAH, you are so holy and beautiful and mighty. I praise your name because you alone are worthy of all praise. I fell in love with your kindness and mercy. Oh YAH, your love for me is deeply moving. When you sent YAHshua, you sent the greatest gift of all. You sent your love wrapped in a manger; you sent a precious part of you. Abba YAH, touch my tongue and heart and soul. Bless me to be an effective witness for you so that the world may know that there is only one Creator, the true Creator, YAH Almighty.

Majestic King and everlasting Creator, I want to worship at your feet. I want to love you; you make my life complete. YAH you are the dream maker, promise keeper, and trustworthy friend. I am so thankful that you have chosen to lend your hand to someone sinful and lower than the dust. You decided to take me as I am, and for that, for your love, for your desire to see me free, I give to you every single part of me to do as you will. I will go where you lead, and witness the precious name of YAH through your Son, our Savior, YAHshua, I choose to be a witness for you forever. Forever your witness, Jabari Khalfani Woods. For YAH's glory in YAHshua's holy name to the glory of YAH I pray, HalleluYAH!

Dedication

This collection of poetry is actually my heart and soul on paper. I have been touched by YAH, the King of heaven and earth. Let the words of my mouth and the meditation of my heart be acceptable in YAH's sight, my Rock and my Redeemer.

I dedicate this collection of psalms to YAH'S glory; in loving memory of my dad Moses Woods Sr. and my mom Bonnie; my beautiful wife Kimberly; my siblings Afreya, Kamilah, and Akeem; and to my children to come and future generations. These precious souls have been crucial parts of all the chapters in my life. And I thank YAH for your faithfulness, love, friendship, and wisdom.

Be Inspired!

Contents

Getaway

Cast away your fears of degradation,

And revive your spirit for the search

Of a new revelation.

No pointed sticks to poke your spine

But an untold story that will capture the minds

Of every mortal who walks, talks, and breathes.

Across the galaxy of misconception

Lie the hearts of the forgotten.

Smitten with the taste of freshly colored, fiery roses,

This poses as a symbol for all humankind

Of paths laid waste at the hands of human displeasure.

Carefully distorted and supported by the evil hand

Of he who fell from the holy land

In search of minds to unravel, souls to devour

And shower with endless pain

Pouring down like acid rain,

Flowing for all eternity.

Whirlwinds swirl in a perfect motion

As the sun sings to the ocean.

A soft melody of soon-to-be rest,

Calling on all who have been chosen to pass the test.

I sing in praise as the holy one of Israel raises the dead

In search of one, even two standing

To welcome his blessed return for all

Who have suffered and mourned.

A sinner I am until the day I win my life—

Sacrifice, sacrifice, sacrifice
Worldly possessions, sin at my own

Discretion, lust for fame, money,

And wealth,

Not projected for the betterment

Of self.

Hopefully, in time one will be able to see

That the true wealth is to be blessed

With a family

Who inspires, desires, and searches to be free

Mentally, spiritually, and physically.

Thank YAH for that mother who prays

Diligently for the sake of all

For with prayer one will never fall.

Thank YAH for that father who has fought

With endless sweat and tears,

Reminding generations after to never fear

Any human being on the face of this earth

For all will one day work for YAH.

Long live the queen who manages to avoid

The sinful nature of man for what you possess

Is more precious than a ruby chest

Full of diamonds and gold.

Long live the king who maintains

Dignity of self, of spirit.

Please hear it, fear it,

And keep YAH's Word close to your heart,

And never let YAH get away.

Thunderstorm

A window opens in heaven on the latter part of a thunderstorm.

A young lady discovers her value and races to uncover the meaning behind the reason she was born.

An earthquake shakes the Midwest on Friday, and a spiritual awakening attacks the dry spirit of complacency.

Why does the moon come out at night?

Why does wisdom hide itself behind painful trials?

I have come airborne, descending from an invisible helicopter.

I landed in the jungle and now live among the wild beast of sin.

YAH, rescue me from this pit I have fallen in.

A window opens in heaven on the latter part of a thunderstorm.

A synoptic story of the same glory, a resurrected life of one,

Directs humankind to look up and not down.

YAHshua destroyed Satan's hold and broke up his hollow ground.

No storm is too powerful.

No threat is too severe.

YAH Almighty sits so high but so near.

An earthquake shakes the Midwest on Friday, and as I dream, YAH's spiritual hands anoint my body.

Blessed be the name of YAH Almighty.

The moon comes out at night because in Genesis, YAH wanted a lesser light to highlight his amazing power to create.

Wisdom illuminates and shows itself worth the wait, like a long-awaited kiss from a long-lost love.

A Timeless Love Song

The unexplainable beauty that arrives at dawn has delivered a timeless love song with cords of heavenly strings and royal blue, like seams. A portrait frame unlocks stories of history's birth pains at an anonymous author's appeal, which scattered recklessly to find answers to heal, reveal a departed sequence of a prophetic story. Dreams of heights unreachable, love untamed by time, divine trilogy of harps' melodies strumming in a new time, a new genesis. A true love unblemished from the beginning.

Awaiting honor, praising glory of tomorrow's place in eternity's race toward the finish line. Take a deep breath and close your eyes; make a wish, and allow your soul to rise to new heights. Swimming in the ocean of paradise, sipping new wine on the landscape of the universe. YAH whispering in your ear, softly telling you how special you are. Climbing your heart like a steep mountain slope, striving to reach you at the top of your empire. Father YAH, you are the only one who understands the song of my spirit. YAH, you are and forever will be a timeless love song playing through eternity.

Soar

Heaven is a sanctuary where our holy YAH dwells; life is a mystery that only the spirit can unveil. Your journey is my journey; walk with me into the light of eternity. Capture those moments, and in victory, you will find living in the light of YAHshua was worth striving for. And with all your might, soar!

Love is a gift that only YAHshua's precious blood could fulfill; emotions have nothing to do with YAH's purpose for you, your spiritual destiny, YAH's divine will. Be still, and in the silence of the night, spread your wings and soar!

Unity is perfect harmony joining hand in hand with the faith of the saints, a universal gathering, singing sweet lullabies with one immaculate voice. Destiny is screaming at you, pleading to you to make a choice. Choose to soar!

The only place that you will always be able to soar is in the presence of YAH; seek him through prayer.

What I See

Step into a world full of mercy and favor,
immediately replaced by quiet but sorrows'
sounds of displace. Captured in a time
when heaven's scent is but light-years away,
undoubtedly consumed by a sinner's getaway.

You see, in this world, only the strong survive. It is very
important that one realizes the escape is complex and
petite, but the reward for survival is measured in the
highest regard. Only the strong will receive the key to
the light but must first face the darkness of this night.

Live, for it is the most important challenge of
all, or gather around to face the other's fall.
No happy ending is guaranteed in this world
but instead, a fulfilled life filled with love,
hardships, friendships, adventure, and truth.

Uncover the meaning behind the battle between good and evil within our time, and you will surprisingly discover the life you live is the same as many others. You are not only walking in the path of great human beings before your time but are mysteriously building spiritual and physical mountains to YAH for potential to climb.

Like diamonds cut in perfect spherical form, you have been wonderfully knitted with a soul inside a royal garment, an earthly uniform. Remember, for every soul put to rest, there is another one waiting patiently to take life's test with a specific purpose, a destiny; this is what I see.

This is dedicated to my family and friends: Always live for YAH in the mighty name of YAHshua, and believe in a better tomorrow, love, power, peace, goodness, truth. Shalom.

My World

In a desperate attempt to escape the cruel reality of this
world

And the agony of memories of my past mistakes

That cloud my mind and tear at my heart over and over
again,

I consciously awake to new signs of wonders

And tiny glimpses of better days.

When the power of light generated by YAH's sunrays

No longer can cause cancer,

When love is carried out to the fullest

With clarity, divine loyalty, and truth,

I imagine a time when murder and crime

No longer determine the title of a generation

Nor describe a season of senseless bloodshed,

Ending in millions of fatalities and fatherless babies.

Shame.

No pain discovered or uncovered in this world—

Only silent hymns of victory songs and sweet fragrances from nature's dew after a brief thundering or lightning has passed through.

When I open my eyes, I see a rainbow of colors piercing the sky.

As bluebirds fly by, they uncover folded messages from above,

Sealed with an eternal kiss YAH sent, timeless and abundant.

I only wish my family's and friends' eyes could behold this place, the glowing smile on my face, and the beauty that surrounds me here in my world.

Language of Time

If I spoke in Japanese, I would deliberately mislead the Portuguese.

If I wrote in Latin, the hoods of Manhattan would convict me of a felony.

You're full of supplements that appear to help your chemical imbalance,

But the truth is, they were never intended to help,

Just make you think you had an advantage.

Lie on, you twisted cartoon villain,

Hiding out, furious and terrified

Because you are rapidly losing your dominion.

So I pray.

Weather predicts a hurricane.

There is a famine in the land as souls descend into hell,

Inescapable quicksand.

Diamonds have become more precious than human beings.

Blood sheds all over Africa;

Children scream, not for the bottle, but for Mom,

Dad, sister, nephew.

Militia has approached and swept through their village;

Rwanda privileged compared to hell.

Light the fire with your gasoline mixture.

Adjust the antenna on your widescreen picture,

And get your mind out of the gutter.

YAH, bless me to be bolder,

Fiercer, and true.

If I spoke the truth, you would refuse to listen.

Listen ... or perish.

Words of Wisdom

Make a wish, and in time, YAH may choose to grant it to you.

Hold on tightly to the voyage that life will take you to.

Open the treasures of your heart, and lock them away in the deep conscience of your mind

That they may be an aid through difficult and tragic times.

Open your eyes to faith in YAH and YAHshua, the son, a new understanding,

Realizing that the pressures of this life can be so demanding.

Heal slowly; speak boldly.

Stand for something bigger, greater than yourself.

Scream when your worst nightmare becomes a reality.

Then gradually climb the ladder to soulful discovery, love, and integrity.

Search like a clever fox scoping out its next prey.

Analyze your mistakes in hopes that tomorrow's choices are better than today's.

Pray for guidance and heavenly solutions.

Meditate, elevate, and most important, acknowledge your potential.

Above all, you see, taste, touch, and experience.

Remember that nothing is greater than the love of YAH.

Life is what you make it to be.

Lessons in the Valley

(Fall 2010)

I have learned the lessons of trust in the school of trial.

I grow weary and teary eyed when I think about how often I have fallen where there was no root to be planted.

I took for granted answers to endless wishes,

Demised wisdom, and attained to earthly elements

Where no might or sign of daylight is present.

Like flickering in the beauty of a crescent moon.

Cradle my ties, tarry in hopes that one day

My soul will rise from the alleyways of perdition.

Lessons in the valley.

Echoes call my name; conscience afflicts my brain.

All a reminder of darker days, when bright afternoons suddenly became midnights.

Clouds stalling my midflight perception, creating pain.

Lessons in the valley.

Quicksand ties my ankles, gradually pulling me further and further down.

Heights appearing to far out of reach to conquer and abound.

Promises, problems, provisions—

In that order in my life have come around.

One life in view of paradise,

Screaming, "Save me,"

When victory paved the way for me.

Early in the morning, input love, and let go

Of my fear; clearly YAH's mercy has kept me here.

Lessons in the valley.

Free will a gift but a curse if used for reproach.

A vigilante escaped of mortal men.

Caged creatures roaring to get in.

The surface of the most secret garden.

Keys, formulas, perhaps the glass globe will predict

My ascension from the deep, hollow pit.
Traveling far from my youth's playground.

The gospel's truth showdown is chasing me further and
further into the wilderness,

Aiming to save me, teach me lessons in the valley.

Legend

(Fall 2012)

To speculate would only underestimate the power of YAH. Rabbinical teachings initiate to flight, dreams as they soar above the foundations of the night. Calm winds usher in eternities' hymns, soft-spoken but mighty in content. Legend.

A spell in a deep water well hides rivers of secrets. Discrete, quiet peace is the tone of this unique melody, which forces me to search with my heart and not my mind, disguising my fear in search of the true me. Legend.

Unspotted, almost as if I never existed, no echo's recorded by the hint of a mockingbird as daunting and painful as a bullet's sting, contrasting the joy foreseen. In the exhilaration of a playground's swings lift off. Legend.

What kings are made of, solid grit, misunderstood misfit, confused by his innate aggression, honored by the mantle he is destined to wear. Redemption allows souls to escape, hellbent on destruction; carefree discussion; opposed by rich, individualistic barbarians with little to no knowledge or understanding of the tides and the glory of a legend.

Roses and Pearls

(Fall 2010)

By the time you read this letter, my dearly beloved,

I will have ascended with the heavenly host on high.

Don't worry if you get lonely at night.

I want you to look deep into the darkness of the sky's starlight,

And there in the beauty of ocean's springs

Are reflections and openings to everlasting dreams.

Sacred scrolls of days foretold there, where familiar faces

Disappear into empty spaces,

Never to be seen again.

Roses and pearls.

Hearts magnified with passion and transparent, enfolding one another into a single lens.

Only to highlight the good times and to reveal the tragedy

Of your pride.

Roses and pearls.

Gentle answers always seem to soften

The intent of hostile questions.

In hope that love's intercession will teach us

Lifelong lessons

That will carry us to the inner beauty

Placed in the souls of virtuous women,

The painful burdens

Placed on the shoulders of real men.

Until we meet again,

Remember the pearls I placed around your neck

As my sign of my love and devotion.

Remember the rose gardens we sat in on our wedding day.

My love, think often of me; I will always remember your smile,

My eternal symbol of joy and a testament to the happy times we shared when we danced among the living.

Roses and pearls. You never know what you have until it's gone.

Anointed

(Fall 2001)

When the sun hits the seas on the ease of September,

My mind begins to take a decline back to an unforgettable place.

A bitter taste brushes the inner layer of my lip.

Poison and distaste cause an allergic reaction.

As images flash back and forth,

Steadfast, I try my best to stay on course.

I race to the scene of yesterday's dream.

And envision a flower, which captures the former and now broken roots of New York's tower.

A shower of misery and distress forces us all to confess

Our secret ways, our earthly praise of man.

Now no one will stand the wrath of uncompromising fury.

Deliberate as is most of humankind's sin,

Delivering pain to all who are captured within

This season; no reason to give in

When everyone around me has fallen at the hands of sin.

Over the mountains some have seen the end to the confusion, YAH's perfect provision and expertise.

You are walking dead and do not know it, living a wasteful life,

Forgetting all about the price that YAHshua paid

When he died and laid

With the burden of your lies.

The torment when one dies.

The endless cries of the innocent.

YAH is omnipotent.

Truly, truly, truly anointed.

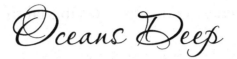Oceans Deep

(Fall 2002)

Ocean's deep, mountain peaks

Are not able to contain you in any element beyond the ceiling's sky.

Dreams repeat in attempt to break this shell and fly

Above without limit, without distraction.

Soulful interaction makes one choose hope, makes one choose life.

Ideally, real love cannot be manipulated, demeaned, or tagged with a price.

Underline counterschemes and earthly means of true devotion

And careless reaction to one's fragile emotions

And freeze time—ticktock, ticktock.

Still life forces one to rewrite their purpose.

Beginning plans interrupted by habitual sinning,

This forces one to give in.

Inability to capture one's thoughts,

Chaos, refusal to be taught,

Refusing to be identified with yourself.

So I continue on, blessed with the utterance to poetically reveal

My heavenly Father's will for his fallen doves.

Outside looking in, things appear rather bleak.

The pit of hell has buried many deep, and time is running out

To freely receive YAH's gift, abundant gift, YAH's utterance; this is YAHshua.

Vibrant and alive, I have finally discovered the reasons so many fall, so many cry, so many die; they let the meaning of life pass them by and in a blink of an eye.

There, no longer standing, our Savior is only demanding that we give just a little back for all his suffering and pain he so boldly proclaimed for you and me.

In due time, all humankind will find that the life we live was all to the glory of his.

I miss you, YAH; I miss you, peace.

In time, you will allow my soul to be released to you for eternity. Oceans deep.

Still Standing

(Winter 2011)

It all begins with a firm transformation of the mind

Followed by a deep-rooted awareness of the desperately wicked times

We have arrived in.

Why then do we hook on to sin like bait?

Mistake the truth for a lie and inwardly die, without igniting any sense of anger or shame from the flames that spark and with force to pull our souls apart.

In my heart, I render biblical truths to be the only shield that is able to guide and protect and seal my eternal destiny.

Throughout this trial of other's cultural denial,

Their own self-saving grace and deliberate attempts

To all but erase any trace of lineage, custom, hope.

I boldly forge on, gifted with the ability to cope.

With the frequent false portrayals that seek to destroy and prevail against the testimony of my soul and the confinement that blinds those who are unaware that they are wearing invisible veils.

That keeps them wondering if there is more to me than their hidden eyes are able to see.

Knowledge of self has knitted a unique stamina within me, and I owe it all to the one and only YAH Almighty.

Thanks to you Oh Ancient of Days, my mother has blossomed in her golden days, my sisters have matured into beauties beyond description, and my brothers are still able to conquer the myriad storms that come their way. Still standing.

Homecoming

(Fall 2012)

Where have the years gone? Inwardly awaiting the rising of a new dawn on a horizon escape? We place our troubles at your throne, terrified, trapped in an ancient war zone, where battle collides from a supernatural level, as hell's army attempts to move to center stage.

YAH's heavenly host position in praise, preparing for the coming of the messianic age. You are invincible, the one and only, the Ancient of Days, the eternity keeper, the guide that orders my ways.

Highlight your strength in and through me; direct my thoughts, be my shield, and lead your people to victory. You are the author and lover of my soul, the dream maker, the Rose of Sharon.

Home seems so far away and distant from me. I have rebelled, commitments failed, tossed like a broken sail floating in the mist of the ocean. I have overcome by the favor of your mercy, water and fire, painful trials that have rained down shame like a flood. What's left is a broken spirit, a vessel beaten, withered, and torn, merely existing, no fight left, struggling, holding on to my last breath, begging to be released from this culture of death. Return to me, and renew my strength; grant me entrance into your heavenly rest. This I write on this cool fall night to you, Most High, asking to come home.

The letters on the page are decoded with subliminal messages asking Almighty YAH to take me deeper into his love, pavilion, and secret place. I love Abba YAH. The breath you have given me, may I breathe praises to you through eternity. The passion you have given me, may it transform the wicked and quicken the righteous. The light you have given me, may it always sit elevated on a hill for all to see. YAH, you have placed a flame in me so hot, so passionate, so consumed with love for you. May this torch always burn for you.

Eternity

(Summer 2012)

I was once lost; now I am found, rooted out of the sinful bounds of evil.

Listen closely, my people, quivering effortless to endure, for it is a must to trust and obey the true Word of YAH Almighty.

No doubt I am no longer subjected to fear.

Out of this world, my soul will rise and reappear

In marble-like manner, without a scar, a glitch.

Watch your actions, and measure carefully your soul's response.

And prepare your spirit for YAH's Word, which is stronger than an avalanche.

Eternity.

Are you listening? Will you be able to hold firm and maintain sanity?

When all humanity will be forced to face the pain

Of a dying world?

Corroded with the deep impression of sin,

Polluted skies, and deadly lies that hide within the human mind.

Will you take the time to free your mind away?

So you can save your soul and let your loved ones know that hope is only a prayer away.

Today, at a moment, there will be no other to question, to uncover the truth of the Messiah's armor, which is stronger than bulletproof.

Untouched, undefiled, the maker of your human profile is coming for you.

Ready or not, he will fulfill the plot of the story and send you somewhere for eternity.

The Connection on This Bridge

(Wednesday, September 17, 2008)

Freedom bells are coming down that dusty road, shallow shells once hardened now soft enough for the captives to break free. Dim the lights in the room, and invite those seeking to escape this world in for prayer.

I escape when I fold my hands and fall upon my knees. YAH, you take my thoughts of you and align them in a heavenly language that only my spirit can understand. You set me free to get up again after a battle with horrendous sin that tries, tries so hard to entangle me again.

Political unrest grips the nations, who are frightened by the impending spiritual, social, and economic doom. Waves from Katrina brush through like jet-black oil newly discovered within the borders of our own countries. That is, if it were possible.

Achievement is recognized on a world stage that highlights sin and compromise. The wisdom of the elderly is no longer honored; most men are considered to be part time fathers, who can no longer provide lifelong gifts—such as time—to their sons and daughters.

The connection on this bridge is a loose foundation that eventually will fold and crumble into the water. Massive souls frantically seek shelter at the top of the tower.

Conspiracy, the original investigation commits systematic suicide every time it bends the rules in order to tell the public the truth.

In review, let's repeat the subliminal theme again.

Freedom bells are coming down that dusty road.

I escape when I fold my hands and fall upon my knees.

Political unrest grips the nations.

Achievement is recognized on a world stage.

The connection on this bridge.

Harvest

(October 1, 2007, 9:24 a.m.)

Last night the wind breathed on me, followed by the former and latter rain, a promise fulfilled by YAH Almighty. The light of heaven YAH's impartation of at- one-ment. The galaxy comforts the stars that remind the souls of those who are waiting for the holy visitation. Come, Oh Yisreal, come again to your Father. The celebration that is about to unfold was destined for our time centuries earlier, foretold that one day Yudah would grab hold of the ancient holy scepter. The cycles of Almighty YAH have come full circle, and now all will see YAH's majesty and glorious wonder in YAHshua's holy name. Take a minute. Take a moment to breathe. It's harvest time.

Convinced

(Fall 2007)

I am justified and saved by faith through favor alone.

I no longer have to ponder my salvation, questioning if YAH really has a home for me in heaven.

I am certain that YAH sees me before I seize the moment of repentance, or a soft sincere apology that attempts to express the deep pain and shame when I tell the Most High that I am sorry.

YAH's love for me is so deep.

I am no longer confident in my aspirations to be a better man.

I can close my eyes and know that no matter what, YAH will keep the world turning on its axis.

I have several days when my confidence praises my short-lived moments of spiritual consistency.

The integrity I desire within my heart inspires my spiritual conscience to stay the course.

I am not impressed with the spurts of motivation.

I want to be bold all of the time, not just when my days are laced with smiles and sunshine.

I have to question my questions of faith, power, and joy, which only interrogate my own conscience, searching endlessly, looking for the answer.

I want to launch a healing campaign where YAH and YAH alone leads the praise and worship.

I want to love the way YAH intended it to be.

I want to walk in the coolness of the garden without shame or separation from the Genesis before Genesis became disappointed with man.

Adam's wish and heavens favorable response.

I am significant; that's what I hear my soul say.

I argue with this hell-driven flesh, and then I realize that my spirit already won over two thousand years ago.

Make mention of me in your prayers, my mediator and high priest; when you communicate with the Almighty, will you deliver this letter for me?

I want YAH to know that I will never stop trying to crucify my flesh and conquer the carnal thoughts of my mind and body.

I want YAH to know that I am thankful, so thankful that his mercies are renewed for me personally every morning.

I want to spell out the word "love" and whisper songs of pure love and devotion, and I want to speak in just the right spirit for YAH Almighty. YAH, these are my thoughts, my inner sanctuary, my soul.

Please note them in your Book of Life, and when you think of me, may the thought of my life put a smile on your face.

In YAHshua's holy name I pray to the glory of Abba YAH.

Confound the Wise

(Fall 2012)

I am talking, but no one seems to be listening. I live in two dimensions and have been granted access to YAH's heavenly gate. I have entered the wars of ancient times and have seen the paths of past victors' glory decline.

Confound the wise.

Love and redemption prepared my preordained ascension into heaven when I dream.
I prevail by the mighty power of the Author of life, and through the steps of his Son, our Savior YAHshua, I have been invited back home to Eden, the Fertile Crescent, YAH's paradise.

Confound the wise.

Choose this day who you will serve. I observe the reluctance of the man or woman who hears my words, but refuses to believe in the true Creator of heaven and earth. The gospel's proclamation altogether ignored, although I have continually rehearsed its truth in entirety.

Confound the wise.

Unlocking mysteries that have for centuries fascinated the minds of men, and discovering biblical truths so profound and so powerful with one intention—to put a complete end to the dominion of sin's influence on a fallen world. Gold freezes into transparent glass, paved in diamonds so bright the sun appears like the lesser light. I exhale and meditate on the precepts of YAH's commands. I concentrate on YAH's real spiritual intent, and with joy and Bible in hand, I raise his words toward the sky, never questioning why, YAH chose to use the foolish things of this world to

Confound the wise.

At the Top of the Mountain

(Sunday, August 30, 2008)

Clear water flows inside the falls of pure love; redeeming power cools the tides of doubt, confusion, and fear,

At the top of the mountain.

Wondering admiration of beauty unexplainable to the human mind, impossible to verbalize with human words,

At the top of the mountain.

Showers of endless serene moments are captured at the top of the mountain, where I encountered the Eternal One, the Maker of existence,

At the top of the mountain.

I want you and desire your affection; the lessons you teach are the answers to all life's questions. It is you, Oh Mighty YAH, who holds the key,

At the top of the mountain.

Salvation, you rescued me from such a deep darkness, fire continually burning around me. And all at once, the world and everything in it took last place in my life, as you turned my focus on you. I am in love, and it feels too good to be true, and I know that all good and perfect gifts come from YAH, who communicates from the heavens above.

At the top of the mountain.

Perhaps, you have uncovered the most precious secret of all. That in our human weakness, when we are at our worst, it is then that you are at your best, willing to teach us through love and spiritual tests.

At the top of the mountain.

Wherever you may be at this moment, YAH is speaking as far as the east; YAH is speaking as far as the west, the north, and the south. Stand up, and with one accord, let all the inhabitants of the earth shout, "YAH, we are sorry for forgetting you are the only source that sustains, creates, the only one who deserves our admiration, our praise."

At the top of the mountain.

YAH, you alone deserve the glory. Forgive us, and return us to you. Teach us your ways and show us our purpose. We miss you, we need you, we confess our sins, we accept your gifts, we believe in your Son—our Savior, YAHshua—and we promise to do what you have called us to do

At the top of the mountain.

YAH's Letter

(Saturday, December 22, 2007)

Let me take you to a place where happiness is not found in the abundance of things but in your spirit's ability to believe without seeing. I am a sword dipped in YAH's holy oil; I am an ocean, deep blue and royal. YAH's letter. I want my children to love me and me alone. I want my daughters to value their temples and remain pure amid temptation. I want my sons to know that they are created in my image and must uphold me in their words and conduct. Endless centuries have swept through the ages like the pages of a never-ending story. I love you deeper than any meaning you can conceive. The journey of life is orchestrated by my hands; leave my children alone. I hear the screams of righteous Abel, and I have prepared a place for all my children to join me at my table. Praise me in the morning, and call on me throughout your day. And in each moment, reflect on my presence that is always present to direct and guide your way. Let me take you to a place where happiness is not found in the abundance of things, but in your spirit's ability to believe without seeing. I am a sword dipped in YAH's holy oil. I am an ocean, deep blue and royal. YAH's letter.

A Description

(August 26, 2008, 11:27 a.m.)

Against all odds you shot up from the depths of the pit; like Aaron's rod, you blossomed and sealed the beginning of harvest. Rapture ready, a long way from street gangs, drugs, childhood pranks, and high school love you blossomed.

A form of a figure that was and is and shall ever be, the son of YAH, shining like the sun in its splendor. A portrait painted with heavenly colors, piercing shapes flowing effortlessly like the folding and unfolding wings of a butterfly.

Elevating higher and higher until just in reach of the third heaven, fulfillment of a cycle that concludes one sad song and the reconciling command by YAH to cleanse the temple and usher in the great exodus home.

Saints assemble to behold the end-time ingathering of epic proportions. Trumpet sounds as lost souls tremble in fear, a brief description of things to come.

Strange Worship

Contained in a huge synagogue, immersed in false
worship and paganism,
You remain contained as a religious slave, entangled in a
fellowship of demons. For a moment, your soul screams
there is something here that is just not right, but after
the sermon and offering passes through, you remain
beguiled from the words of a false prophet who cleverly
persuades you.
Strange worship.

The local clergy is convinced that you're spiritually blinded,
therefore, you will never investigate who they really
worship behind the wall. Nations claim your inheritance,
but you cannot see that far, because your mind is so
consumed with appeasing human-made traditions, that
have carried many self-proclaimed preachers to perdition.
Strange worship.

The answer your soul needs is just a prayer in front of
you, but the dark complexion of the messenger's skin and

the anointed tongue he speaks in sounds like a foreign language, unknown to your now-conquered mind. At the throne of your heart sits idols, not the true king. I must be careful with my tone, or you will surely cast a stone, and mistake my pure intent for blasphemy.
Strange worship.

The environment needs less pollution, but the earth, a living organism, does not depend on humans to clean the galaxy. The true source is hidden from you because your reality only consists of the things that are seen, not of the things that appear.
Strange worship.

Status has become more important than the simplistic contentment of knowing where your soul will go when YAH commands to take your breath. The audience applauds your flowery words and upholds you over YAH's Word. The tragedy within the tragedy of a stiff-necked people, who relish in the created, and not the Creator of heaven and earth, is that they are so spiritually sick and arrogant to see that they are rejecting their birthright, a heavenly life, for the pleasure of sin that will only last for a season. You are caught up in Strange worship.

You do not know who you serve.

The Final Curtain Call

(Monday, September 22, 2008, 8:40 p.m.)

Move out of my way. I am running fearlessly to the arms of YAH Almighty. Remember me as the silent witness who whispered the truth in your ear. YAH appears in the midst of our time. From America to the Middle East, millions fall to their knees, shocked and desperately seeking cover. Uncover your day of visitation has met you like a thief in the night.

The final curtain call.

The opera echoes sounds as the final curtain flows together. The weather predicts hurricanes as orphans on the coast run for shelter. Family members, hugging and weeping, knowing that this will be the last moment they will be able to spend together.

The final curtain call.

Military equipment malfunctions; bullets refuse to be released from the cannon of fire, and armies grow in anger and fatigue. The confederates against the Most

High drop their weapons and fall to their knees as they wave the white flag, screaming, "I surrender."
The final curtain call.

The quick light flashes from east to west. The holy one of Y'isreal rides the clouds to the mountain where his feet will rest. No protest, no sound of a jury deliberating whether they will convict the innocent to death. No more pain, sharks, or chains, no more oppression.
The final curtain call.

Adam has learned his lesson, Eve has renewed her vows, and YAH returns in the coolness of the garden. The abyss opens its jaws and swallows Satan and all his legions of demons. Closed case. A finished race. A finished story. Abba YAH receives the glory. The kingdoms of this world have become the kingdoms of our YAH!
The final curtain call.

Shower Me, Oh YAH

(Wednesday, September 1, 2010, 9:49 a.m.)

Shower me, Oh YAH with your love again.
Mend my broken heart because I am breaking hearts that
I want to see whole.
Allow me to cherish you, Most High YAH, more and
more; remove the demons from my life, and once again,
open the door to my heart.

A sinful habit or addiction searching for the real cure, it
is you, Oh YAH, my prescription. YAH, is it me who is
hindering my family from reaching its spiritual destiny?
YAH, I am doubling over. YAH, I am sick and in pain.
Depression grips me when I meditate on the rain of trials.
Frequently, I want to go where you are, precious YAH,
in prayer in an attempt to connect. YAH, I thank you
for touching my heart last night and giving me hope
again. I want to live my life the way you intended, but
I am grieved when I hear the ugly truths about myself.
YAH, I am disconnected from my family. I feel alive and
dead at the same time. Oh YAH, I ask you everything

because you are my everything, and I know YAH can do anything, anything.

Fear and anxiety—or maybe doubt and curiosity—led me to a place in the desert of my soul where there were no signs of rescue or a refreshing water stream.

YAH, I am screaming inside. I fail and hide. I run and isolate myself at times, finding it difficult to verbalize the torment my mind, body, and soul has been feeling. YAH, I want to live again-free to laugh, free to cry, free to love, free to fly, free to share your endless love for me and all humanity.

YAH, I made a mistake. I attempted to uncover true love without you, and as a result, my spirit runs in circles. I continue to practice what is wrong and unholy in your sight. I am worse than weak. I need you, Oh Mighty YAH to pick me up and put me back on my feet, and strengthen me, Oh YAH, like Daniel in the vision with Gabriel. YAH, I thank you for allowing me to communicate with you in heaven. In YAHshua, I make my problem known unto you. YAH, thank you for not forsaking me. Thank you, YAH, for not destroying me or hurting me.

Shower me, Oh YAH, with your love again. Mend my heart because I am breaking hearts that I want to see whole. Allow me to cherish you, Most High YAH, more and more. Remove the demons from my life, and once again, open the door to my heart.

I need a revelation, a spiritual healing. Make me over, Oh YAH. Fill in my spiritual blemishes, and give me joy in the inward part, so that I can sing again. Oh YAH, I only have one life to live; remove oppression, deception, and put me back together again. Sometimes, Abba YAH, my king, I feel like my heart's in the ground, and my soul has been kidnapped by the woes and lusts of this world.

Shower me, Oh YAH, with your love again. Mend my heart because I am breaking hearts that I want to see whole. Allow me to cherish you, Most High YAH, more and more. Remove the demons from my life, and once again, open the door to my heart.

Oh YAH, help me to overcome.

O Precious Gatekeeper and Ruler of All

(Monday, November 7, 2011, 9:44 a.m.)

It is with tears, awe, and admiration I give my life to you Oh Precious Gatekeeper and Ruler of all.

It is with fear and excitement I collapse before YAH's throne, eagerly awaiting a favorable response, answers to my questions, and a provision for my home. It is with deep sorrow I confess my sins, my conscious choice to do wrong. Sometimes I sing a praise and worship psalm, to somehow get into the ear of the Most High YAH. But whether I sing loudly or whisper softly, YAH is always there to love and remind me that the battle will never stop. I desire to love YAH with every part of me. YAH reaches down and touches me in the most inward part of my soul.

I give my all, my resources unto YAH, as a sacrifice of praise. Malachi Chapter 3 reminds me of this when offering to YAH the right way. Abba YAH, save the children who are being murdered every day in the womb. Abba YAH, set the captives free; return and plant your feet upon this land. Abba YAH, forgive me for thinking too highly of myself. Oh YAH, forgive me for holding back from you what is yours to give. YAH, let me build your altar. Let me live free in you; let me be used as an instrument of peace to inspire, encourage, defend, and protect your people.

Abba YAH, in my physical body, I am so afraid of heights, but in my spirit, I want to fly as high as your favor and mercy will let me. Abba YAH, grant my request so I can use your overflow to help others, to bless.

It is with tears, awe, and admiration I give my life to you. It is with tears, awe, and admiration I give my life to you, Oh Precious Gatekeeper and Ruler of all.

And in giving with joy and absolute faith, I have given nothing because you made me, you called me, you honored me, you transformed me, and you made it all.

Is It Wrong? Sequel

(Monday, March 22, 2010, 8:16 a.m.)

Is it wrong because I see the gifts that YAH has put in you? Is it wrong because I believe that you are more important than you think you are?

Is it wrong because I believe your soul is more beautiful than your smile?

Will you accept my gift as a token of love and my appreciation of your conversation?

Why was I born? I know the answer to that—to inspire all people to seek Abba YAH and the vast treasure YAH has placed within them.

I sing sometimes because I am trying to uncover this beauty, this holy melody; I am trying so hard in my own words to describe the magnificence and power and wisdom of Almighty YAH.

Is it wrong to dream of flying? Is it wrong to cry for the innocent who cannot protect themselves? Shelter me, Oh

YAH from the storm. Make my life count. I don't want to live like the norm. YAH, inspire me because I know deep down I am nothing without you. YAH, bless me to fund my family's journey home.

Is it wrong to seek what is invisible and love what most call unlovable?

I love the story of the knight in shining armor, sent to rescue the damsel in distress. YAH, make me a man after your own heart, and maybe then—only then—will I be satisfied, as you give me more and more of you.

Coming out of the sun in amazing formation, beholding the Hamachiah with my spiritual eyes, being swept up high into the heavens.

Abba YAH Almighty, I am in love with you.

Is it wrong to want to be YAH's best, YAH's choice, YAH's most prized possession?

Is it wrong to want to sing more, be more, search more, love more for YAH?

YAH, will you inspire me again, and again, and again?

YAH, will you use me to manifest one of your most incredible works in your earth?

YAH, will you talk to me no matter my circumstance, mistakes, heartache, or fear? YAH, show me your glory. Allow me to sit at your feet as you tell me the story of how you created it all.

YAH, I am so human. YAH, I am so wonderfully and fearfully made by you.
YAH, I am so weak, so insecure, so vulnerable, so different. So created in the image of you.

Is it wrong because I see the gifts that YAH has put in you?

Is it wrong because I believe that you are more important than you think you are?

Is it wrong because I believe your soul is more beautiful than your smile?

Is it wrong?

Oh Precious YAH, I am in a battle. My heart and spirit feel like fire. I am in deep mediation, praising and reminiscing on past victories YAH, has given me, victory after victory over my carnal desire.

YAH, I need your help. Remove the demon that is trying to quiet my heart, my soul, and my mind.

YAH, I need a new start. YAH, I am in desperate need of spiritual surgery. YAH, I need a new heart. Windows of emotion flood my body every time I think of what you, Oh YAH, have done for me. Lately, I have been inspired to say something, sing something, do something with meaning.

Make me all over again, Oh YAH. Take me somewhere beautiful in the spirit; make me understand the privilege of tasting your honey, your precious word.
YAH, will I always fail you? Or do you foresee a time in my life when I will completely surrender my selfish will, my way for YAH's way?

YAH, Oh Mighty, Sovereign King, you have the ability to read the hearts of every human being. YAH, what is my soul saying? What song is my heart playing? I am dying inside, and I need YAH and no one else to give me direction.
YAH, I have grieved. I have grieved and retreated into an opaque veil, where I attempt to hide my conscience from you. YAH, I am in so much turmoil. I feel so much spiritual pain. I have become vain—so carnal, so earthly.

Is it wrong because I see the gifts that YAH has put in you?
Is it wrong because I believe that you are more important than you think you are?

Is it wrong because I believe your soul is more beautiful than your smile?

Is it wrong?

Sequel.

Q & A

(Summer 2012)

Abba YAH, why do I always expect your best when I give you my worst? I feel the reaping of the sowing from my selfish, carnal ways. Oh my YAH, forgive me, my Precious King, for hurting you, and your children and myself.

I want to see clearly, Oh King. YAH, I need your love to press deeply until my heart and soul are pure.

Beautiful melodies, I miss YAH's real love.

YAH, I do not deserve any honor, any blessings, any mercy. But you, Oh YAH, are wonderful to me, so wonderful in spite.

My words are only an excuse to put on paper what my heart and spirit fail to do. I read your commandments, Oh Mighty sovereign YAH,

but run away from them at the slightest yearning of my mind, body, this flesh.

YAH, your Word reads through me so easily, revealing my true character, uncovering every spiritual deficiency.

YAH, what am I searching for? YAH, does the mind of my spirit really scream for more of you?

Touch me again, Oh King. Rescue me again. YAH, you are my everything.

YAH, I want to be pure for you. YAH, I want to be honest, trustworthy, and true.

YAH, I am so lonely, so unbelievably careless. YAH, my heart beats to make everything right in my life again.

YAH, how can I let things go, people go, failure go?

YAH, teach me to listen to your heartbeat. Grant me your wisdom. Make my life complete again and again. In YAHshua's holy name, I pray to the glory of Abba YAH, HalleleuYAH!

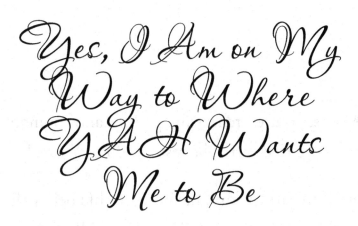

Yes, I Am on My Way to Where YAH Wants Me to Be

(July 4, 2010, 12:54 a.m.)

Yes, I am on my way to where Almighty YAH wants me to be. Heaven's gates open up for me to a place I dream of and read about in the deep pages of YAH's scriptures, rehearsing psalms, and triumphant songs that birth the restoration of Y'isreal. Completely embracing the righteous road we have been chosen to embark upon, covered by the blood of the Lamb and rejoicing in the victory that YAHshua has won. The glory of YAH—the recorded sounds of a community singing Hosanna— echoes abound as the entire world praises YAH from the ocean floor to the hilltops of the highest mountain.

Yes, I am on my way to where YAH wants me
to be. Heaven's gates open up for me to a place
I dream of and read about in the deep pages of

YAH's scriptures, rehearsing psalms, and triumphant songs that birth the restoration of Y'isreal.

Farewell to earthly love, memories of life below the sky horizon, lusts of temporal pleasures engulfed in crowded places drowning in the deceit of Babylon. So long envy, fear, and pain. No more restless nights, lies, and shame. Remembered for persevering, honored for always hearing the voice of the majestic YAH guiding me through trials and strife, leading me home, and giving me the power to discern between wrong and right.

Yes, I am on my way to where Almighty YAH wants me to be. Heaven's gates open up for me to a place I dream of and read about in the deep pages of YAH's scriptures, rehearsing psalms, and triumphant songs that birth the restoration of Y'isreal.

Yes, I am on my way.

About the Author

www.yahsdollarproject.org

Jabari Woods a native of Davenport, Iowa has spent most of his adult years inspiring others to be the best they can be in YAH. A graduate from St. Ambrose University with a Bachelor of Arts in Business Management, and a Masters in Social Work, Jabari fell in love with biblical history and the importance of serving others, which took him on a journey of self-discovery revealing the original Hebraic name of the Creator YAH and his son our savior YAHshua.

Mr. Woods is the founder/CEO of YAH'S Dollar Project a charitable organization that generates funds to help the less fortunate within the community. YAH'S Dollar Project is inspired by the biblical story of the messiah, YAHshua, who fed 5,000 people with five loaves of bread and two fish. Our mottos is, "Give a little, change the world." YAH'S Dollar Project mission is to "INSPIRE AND EMPOWER ALL PEOPLE TO GIVE THROUGH A COLLECTIVE EFFORT OF MONETARY DONATIONS IN ORDER TO MEET THE NEEDS OF THOSE WITHIN THEIR OWN COMMUNITIES."

"My vision is for every school in the World to have a fund for kids and families to get financial resources. It's a way to empower people economically and help schools become education/social service institutions."

Jabari has over 18 years of professional experience working in the areas of HR, Equity, and Social Services. He continues his mission of servant leadership by creating a positive professional atmosphere for employees, community members, and students to work and grow. Jabari believes, "Through words comes writing, and through writing comes the ability to communicate through our thoughts and feelings. All this takes place in the picking up of a book." Be inspired!

Thoughts / Notes

Thoughts / Notes

Thoughts / Notes

Thoughts / Notes

Thoughts / Notes

Thoughts / Notes

Thoughts / Notes

Printed in the United States
By Bookmasters